MASTERING THE MIND OF MACHINES:

Strategies For Controlling Advanced AI Thinking Machines

Valuable insights into the development, application, and management of AI systems

DR. Selva Sugunendran

CEng, MIEE, MCMI, CHt, MIMDHA, MBBNLP, MGONLP

#1 Best Selling Author, Speaker & Coach

© www.AIRoboticsForGood.com

MASTERING THE MIND OF MACHINES:

Strategies For Controlling Advanced AI Thinking Machines

Valuable insights into the development, application, and management of AI systems

Reading through this book is like sailing a powerful yet responsive vessel on a great river called AI. The river is immense, sometimes capricious. It takes us where it will, and its course reflects an enormous range of human experience and knowledge. Our vessel is humanity's companioning partnership with AI, shaped by both innate human values and our joint project of using the technology as a powerful but finite tool to expand that humanity. We face some risks in travelling this river together, but this also means that there are great rewards for exploration. – Max Raymond

Copyright © 2024 by DR. Selva Sugunendran
"Mastering the Minds Of Machines"

All rights reserved. No part of this book may be reproduced or transmitted in any form or by any means, electronic or mechanical, including photocopying, recording, or by any information storage and retrieval system, without permission in writing from the Copyright owner.

Medical Disclaimer: The author of this book is a competent, experienced writer. He has taken every opportunity to ensure that all information presented here is correct and up to date at the time of writing. No documentation within this book has been evaluated by the Food and Drug Administration, and no documentation should be used to diagnose, treat, cure, or prevent any disease.

Any information is to be used for educational and information purposes only. It should never be substituted for the medical advice from your doctor or other health care professionals.

We do not dispense medical advice, prescribe drugs, or diagnose any illnesses with our literature.

The author and publisher are not responsible or liable for any self or third-party diagnosis made by visitors based upon the content of this book. The author or publisher does not in any way endorse any commercial products or services linked from other websites to this book.

Please, always consult your doctor or health care specialist if you are in any way concerned about your physical wellbeing.

Contents

This structure would aim to deliver a high-level holistic overview of the realities and nuances inherent in the issues of controlling the thinking machines called AI. It should explore different dimensions of AI, from the technical to the social and philosophical, and thereby provide readers with deep and balanced insights into a technology at the heart of our future.

Foreword vii

Preface xiii

CHAPTER ONE: Introduction: The New Frontier of AI Thinking Machines 17

   - Setting the stage for the discussion on AI capabilities, aspirations, and challenges.

CHAPTER TWO: The Architecture of AI Thinking Machines 23

- Exploring the technological infrastructure and design principles of AI systems.

CHAPTER THREE: Programming Intelligence: How AI Learns and Adapts 31

- Understanding machine learning algorithms and adaptive systems.

CHAPTER FOUR: From Vision to Reality: Building an AI 39

- Practical steps and technologies involved in creating an AI from scratch.

CHAPTER FIVE: AI in Action: Case Studies of Current Implementations 45

   - Examining existing implementations of AI across various industries.

CHAPTER SIX: The Capabilities of AI: What AI Can and Cannot Do 51

- Defining the limits and potentials of current AI technologies.

CHAPTER SEVEN: Ethics and AI: Moral Considerations in AI Deployment 57

- Discussing ethical implications and responsibilities in AI development.

CHAPTER EIGHT: Safeguarding Humanity: Controls and Safety in AI Design 63

- Methods and protocols to ensure AI safety and reliability.

CHAPTER NINE: Regulation and Policy: Governing the Power of AI 69

- Overview of global regulatory frameworks and policies shaping AI development.

CHAPTER TEN: Preventing AI Autonomy: Techniques to Maintain Control 75

- Strategies to prevent unwanted AI autonomy and ensuring human oversight.

CHAPTER ELEVEN: AI and Employment: Navigating Job Disruption 81

- Addressing the impact of AI on the workforce and economy.

CHAPTER TWELVE: Balancing Power: AI in National Security 87

- Discussing the role of AI in defence and security, and its global implications.

CHAPTER THIRTEEN: Public Perception and Media: Shaping the AI Narrative 95

- Influence of media and public opinion on AI development and acceptance.

CHAPTER FOURTEEN: Future Predictions: Where AI is Heading 101

- Speculating on future advancements and their potential impacts on society.

CHAPTER FIFTEEN: Conclusion: Controlling Our Creations 109

- Summarizing key points and offering thoughts on the future relationship between humans and AI.

All Books Published By Author of This Book 115

Foreword

Navigating the Waters of Change

Over the past two centuries, we lived through numerous disruptions and changes tied to technological advancements. But few of these technologies provoked such excitement, set such rapid change in motion, eroded the old and created the new as quickly as artificial intelligence (AI). We once could only read about AI and other similar technologies in science fiction novels (as James Cameron did in the 1980s) but no longer. Now, AI is affecting all facets of our lives and making efforts to transform the foundations of our society. Therefore, as you begin to read 'Control of Thinking Machines', you are about to learn not only about AI technology and its effects but, even more importantly, the ethical, social, and economic challenges it poses.

Reading through this book is like sailing a powerful yet responsive vessel on a great river called AI. The river is immense, sometimes capricious. It takes us where it will, and its course reflects an enormous range of human experience and knowledge. Our vessel is humanity's companioning partnership with AI, shaped by both innate human values and our joint project of using the technology as a powerful but finite tool to expand that humanity. We face some risks in travelling this river together, but this also means that there are great rewards for exploration.

The Promise of AI

Here's where things get interesting: the very same machines that make life so miserable today could also be the answer to a lot of our problems. AI has the potential to transform health and medicine in ways we can only begin to imagine. It has the potential to provide direct and more accurate diagnoses, managing the databank of each citizen's health risks in real time and proactively recognising problems and offering potential treatments. It could improve the health of cities around the world through smarter, energy-efficient infrastructure that could manage traffic flows. It could provide tailored education online based on the capability and needs of individual students, radically transforming education and making it accessible to many more people around the world.

These are all potential paradigm shifts, not small steps along the path on which we currently stand. And all could address our most pressing problems. The next step – the hard part – is responsibility.

The Responsibility Entrusted to Us

With great power, of course, comes great responsibility, and we who wield this powerful technology must apply it thoughtfully in accordance with our abilities. This book equips you with that knowledge and those insights, so that you can begin to take your place in shaping the future of AI. In addition to covering reasons for optimism and the nuts and bolts of building an AI system, it also looks at the ethics that must guide the development of the technology, and the global implications of the spread of AI, so that the decisions we make will be balanced and informed.

Much of the conversation about AI paints a stark picture of a world torn between dystopian fears and utopian hopes. The picture is far more nuanced, falling somewhere in between. AI, like any tool, contains the cumulative sum of the intentions and values of those who use it. This is why it's so important to talk through the values we want our technologies to express.

The Role of Public Engagement

It means that the people decide the course of AI. The overriding theme of this book is the need for wide-ranging public engagements about the future of AI. When ordinary people participate in the debates about the future of technology, we can ensure that the direction of AI is decided not just by a conversation that spans technologists and policymakers, but that it considers the priorities of humanity. Education, and transparency, are the best remedies; a public less in the dark is a public better placed to make informed choices and lobby for effective policies to ensure that AI is used ethically and benefits us all.

The Call to Action

This foreword is a clarion call. As you read through the book, think not just about the technological and theoretical levers to pull to control AI, but integrate them into the wider picture of what you can personally do – whether you are a developer, a business leader, a policymaker, or an interested citizen – to help create the future we want. The decisions we make now about the path of AI development, deployment and governance will determine the last days of Humanity 1.0.

A Vision for the Future

Imagine a world in which future generations of AI are catalysts for human creativity and ingenuity, not replacements for it. Imagine future generations of AI systems that are designed not just to be efficient, but as implements of ethical action and social good. Imagine a world where the fruits of AI are shared more equitably, and its costs are managed across society together.

Final Reflections

Beyond being a book about AI thinking machines, Controlling AI Thinking machines is a manual for the wise citizen in this age of intelligent technology; it offers not just information, but ideas through which the matter can be thought about, putting the reader in a position to participate in the discourse regarding the issues involved with AI going forward – to become a citizen, taking an active stance and a voice in regarding AI and seeking sensible policies and actions that will make sure that advances happen in ways that fully respect the dignity of the human person.

The path ahead is challenging, yet it is also exhilarating. Fully informed by the most advanced intelligence that we can muster and empowered by the compassionate instincts that may underlie it, we can chart a path toward a tomorrow in AI that we can be proud of, and nurture that path to a future we can genuinely savour. Let's make this an exciting ride.

Max Raymond

Preface

Welcome to the third instalment in my series on Artificial Intelligence, a journey that continues to explore the profound complexities and boundless potential of AI. In this book, "Controlling AI Thinking Machines," we delve deep into the nuances of AI's current capabilities, ethical implications, and prospects, aiming to equip readers with the knowledge and insights necessary to navigate and shape this rapidly evolving landscape.

If you have followed my previous works, you know that my approach to AI is grounded in a balanced perspective that seeks to harness the power of AI while addressing the critical challenges it presents. This volume builds on that foundation, exploring the mechanisms through which AI operates and the frameworks needed to ensure its safe and beneficial integration into society.

For those new to my work, you will find that this book addresses AI from multiple vantage points—technical, ethical, social, and political. It is crafted not only for experts and practitioners but also for lay readers who are curious about the role AI is destined to play in our future.

The six potential titles listed above encapsulate the spirit and scope of this book:

- "Mastering the Mind of Machines: Strategies for Controlling Advanced AI"

- "Beneath the Code: Ethical Control and the Future of Artificial Intelligence"

- "Harnessing the Horizon: Navigating the Future with AI"

- "AI Unchained: Governing the Power of Thinking Machines"

- "The AI Imperative: Controlling the New Intellectual Frontier"

- "Ethics and AI: Steering the Course of Thinking Machines"

Each title reflects a core theme of this work: the imperative to control and ethically guide the development of AI. Whichever title resonates with you, rest assured that the content within these pages addresses the crucial issues at the heart of contemporary AI debates.

In writing this book, I have drawn upon a diverse array of sources and insights—from the latest research in machine learning and robotics to interviews with leading experts in law, ethics, and public policy. The aim is to provide a comprehensive overview that is both informative and thought-provoking, encouraging readers to consider not only what AI can do but what it should do.

As we stand on the brink of a new era marked by digital intelligence, it is more important than ever to foster an informed dialogue about the paths we are taking. The decisions we make today will shape the future of AI and, by extension, the future of humanity. This book is an invitation to be part of that critical conversation—to engage with the ideas and innovations that will define the coming decades.

Thank you for joining me on this journey. Whether you are a technologist, a policymaker, an academic, or simply a concerned citizen, your engagement and insights are vital as we navigate the thrilling and daunting prospects of AI. Together, let us explore how best to control these remarkable machines that we have created, ensuring they serve our collective goals and uphold our highest values.

DR. Selva

CHAPTER ONE:
Introduction: The New Frontier of AI Thinking Machines

On the eve of a new age of technology that will fundamentally alter how we live, work, and relate to each other, perhaps the most defining change will be on the introduction of Artificial Intelligence (AI). Thinking machines – systems capable of learning, reasoning, and making decisions autonomously from humans – at one time were something out of science-fiction; but increasingly their influence in shaping present and future decisions will be pervasive. The purpose of this book, Controlling AI Thinking Machines (2023) is to shed light on this intriguing yet perplexing area of the world where AI meets human ingenuity and control.

And the fast track for this new line of thought has been the incredible speed of AI evolution. AI began simply and has grown incredibly quickly. In the beginning, rudimentary algorithms for pattern recognition were developed, and now we have systems that operate on an increasingly human scale, able to do things that 20 years ago we thought were possible only with our thoughts. We're talking about everything from voice assistants to more sophisticated decision-making machines that, in some cases, not only emulate human thought processes but surpass them. What this untethering of thinking capacity from our own biology portends for our future is an open and sometimes anxiety-ridden question. How do we draw on the power of AI thinking machines, yet keep them tethered to us, proceeding within our ethical frameworks?

Getting our heads around AI, and where it is going, is one of the tougher intellectual challenges of a generation. 'Narrow AI' refers to intelli-gence systems designed to tackle a specific task, such as facial recognition or the internet search engine, which make use of machine learning methods. 'General AI' refers to a system designed to be able to complete any intellectual task a human being can do and, perhaps one day, there will be 'Super Intelligent AI' systems that vastly surpass human intelligence in its own domain. It is quite possible that the route from current AI technologies to more powerful and autonomous AI technologies requires not just technological advances, but better understanding of governance, ethics, and human psychology.

Here we'll take it apart and explore the nuts and bolts that make AI-driven systems operate. We'll dive into the algorithms that serve as the steering wheels, constantly turning the data-laden vehicles of AI-driven systems in new and often transformative directions. We'll dissect the data that powers AI and that in turn is changed by it. We'll look under the hood to see what keeps these systems running. We'll do all that, and more. This book will also investigate the philosophical and ethical issues introduced by the new AI era. Where precisely do we locate the boundaries of machine autonomy? What moral responsibilities do developers have to refrain from or prevent machine-caused harm?

Even more importantly, as AI matures and increasingly become part of our lives, the question becomes less about what works and more about control. The threat that we really have to worry about is that, one day, we might get AI systems that can outsmart us. If that prospect scares you as much as it scares me, then we have to set up safety mechanisms to ensure that these systems do what we want them to do and nothing more. In other words, we need technological safeguards such as kill switches and containment systems, as well as regulation that controls how these systems are configured and deployed.

But, perhaps even more important than any narrowly defined race, are the feedback loops between advances in AI and changes in society. As AI transforms everything from health care and the financial sector to manufacturing, it transforms job markets, privacy norms and the very nature of international security as well. Control of AI is about more than the technology itself; it is about how we shape the technology's role in our society in ways that enhance, not diminish, our humanity.

So, with that serving as an introduction, this first chapter sets the stage for a deeper dive into how to contain an AI thinking machine – with the chapters that follow to serve as a blueprint with respect to how they're built, what they do, how they might come to dominate us, and how to stop them… from us, I hope. Welcome to the world of AI. Like all roads travelled, ours is perilous and foreboding, yet rich and rewarding. Indeed, if there's been one adventure of our modern times that has been thrilling, exhilarating, and filled with the promise of vast untold benefits, while also being loaded with disaster, doom and dangers, it is the journey into AI, which is a technological adventure of dramatic, transcendent and transformative proportions. Let's hope we can keep up. Hopefully we can do it right. But most of all, I ardently trust that in this voyage into the brave new world of AI, we'll never lose our humanity.

CHAPTER TWO:
The Architecture of AI Thinking Machines

Before we can comprehend how to control AI thinking machines, it would help if we understood how they're built. A contributing chapter on AI architecture reveals the essential infrastructure of machine learning. It's the scaffolding of AI systems – built as layers of algorithms and data structures, and designed to emulate the way humans learn, reason, and solve problems. AI systems are made up, not of silicon, but of mathematics: using models and algorithms, machines process data and extract outcomes. This chapter lays out a level of craftsmanship that composes AI – explaining how it's built and how it works.

Foundations of AI Architecture

What's at the core of every AI? Its model, of course – the mathematical model that operates based on data received by the system for input. And although the generic approach used today for machine learning dates to the 1950s, many of the leading 'deep learning' and 'artificial neural networks' (ANNs) now in vogue are modelled on the human brain. ANNs are, in fact, loosely inspired by biology: a system of 'neurons' structured as 'artificial neural networks' with connections between 'neurons' known as 'synapses' (in biological brains), which serve to transfer a signal or 'weighting' from one neuron to the next – or, in technology-speak, from 'node' to 'node'. When the system 'learns', meaning that it 'takes in data to train AI machines to make decisions in similar situations', these weightings – or measurements – are 'altered'.

These models need training, namely, to be exposed to massive amounts of data, which they glean relative relationships from. The process is like how a child can identify an object by being exposed to many instances.

Training can be supervised (the scores are given the right answers when learning), unsupervised (the system needs to identify the patterns by itself) or semi-supervised (a combination between supervised and unsupervised approaches).

Key Components of AI Systems

Data

Data provides the fuel for AI systems. The quality, volume and diversity of data directly affect an AI algorithm's ability to assess or judge a situation with meaningful accuracy. Data must be searched for, gathered, cleaned, and formatted before it can serve as the training set needed to train an AI model. This step must be done right because a data 'blind spot' may mean skewed or 'biased' AI-made judgments that feed and reinforce discrimination (of the target user group) or even garbage in, garbage out.

Algorithms

Algorithms are the decision-making formulas built into AI systems, including single-element rule-based algorithms to more complex multi-layer deep learning networks. The choice of algorithm used to complete a task depends on trying to find the best match between the task at hand, the available data, known signal-to-noise limits, and the computational approach. For example, for pattern-recognition tasks such as recognising speech or images, which typically involve a lot more noise than the signal, deep learning – where datapoints are fed through many layers of hidden nodes to 'learn' the problem on their own – is best.

Hardware

AI systems also need the right hardware on which to run. Advanced graphics processing units (GPUs) and special-purpose chips, such as 'tensor processing units' (TPUs), are often used to handle the huge amounts of data involved in training AI models. The performance and capability of this hardware has a direct impact on the speed and scalability of AI systems.

Design Principles in AI Architecture

Simply building an AI involves more than just putting the pieces together: it also entails adhering to design principles and rules that ensure the system is flexible and robust, and able to achieve what it is supposed to do.

Modularity

Crucially, modularity means that the different parts of the AI system can be developed and tested in isolation before they are brought together – an approach that will greatly facilitate debugging and updates, making the system both hardy (robust) and adaptable (flexible).

Scalability

As the applications of AI expand, ensuring that the systems can scale up becomes a necessity. You've got to make sure that the AI can handle larger loads, larger data without a proportionate amount of slower or otherwise poorer performance.

Transparency

To make AI systems accessible to their users, they should be designed with a capability for transparency that will explain and justify the machine's output – something these techniques aim to provide. Such explanations have application in areas such as healthcare and law.

Challenges in AI Architecture

One of the biggest challenges in AI architecture design is balancing between complexity and intelligibility (or interpretability). More complex models, such as deep neural networks, often perform better but are also considered 'black boxes' because there is little insight into how they make decisions. For this reason, more complex models can pose a challenge when they are applied to critical cases, where reasons behind AI decisions need to be understood.

Another fundamental challenge is security. With AI systems connected to sensitive infrastructure, malicious intrusion becomes a real possibility. Securing these systems requires inoculation against both the data they rely on and model attacks.

Conclusion

The architecture of AI thinking machines is sophisticated and fascinating: it combines state-of-the-art hardware developed by brilliant engineers with state-of-the-art mathematical theories developed by brilliant mathematicians. The resulting systems are capable of learning, improving, adapting, and even thinking. It's crucial to realise that if we hope to control these systems, the first step is to comprehend the architecture. And yet, as we begin to fold AI into different aspects of our society, we must be aware of the principles – and pitfalls – detailed in this chapter, to ensure a utopian future where AI augments human capability without jeopardising human agency.

CHAPTER THREE:
Programming Intelligence: How AI Learns and Adapts

One of the most important things that separates AI from previous styles of computing is its ability to learn and adapt – increasing its ability to drive cars, diagnose diseases, or manage our finances – as it does so. The third instalment in an investigation of these adapting AI thinking machines tells the story of the processes that enable these systems to learn from their environment and experience – and how they modify their behaviour because of that learning.

Learning Paradigms in AI

AIs learn in different paradigms, which is to say, they tackle the problems of acquiring skills and information by engaging in learning tasks well-suited to certain types of tasks and results. The three main types of learning for AIs are supervised learning, unsupervised learning, and reinforcement learning.

Supervised Learning

Training on labelled data (supervised learning), where the model is given the correct output for each input in the training set, is the most common AI paradigm. Labelled data has been widely used in other real-world applications such as image or speech recognition, where the system learns to predict a response from an image or sound by being trained on countless images or sounds labelled with information about their content.

Unsupervised Learning

With supervised learning, the system has labelled outputs to guide it; but with unsupervised learning, there are no labelled outputs, and the AI system has to try to learn what's going on all by itself. This is useful for things like segmenting users based on their behaviour or clustering data to spot unusual patterns — say, for fraud detection in financial transactions, where the system might try to cluster similar transactions to see what normal buying patterns look like, and then flag outliers.

Reinforcement Learning

The behavioural learning model used in reinforcement learning means that the AI must learn how to make decisions by acting and receiving rewards or punishments. Think of training your pet with a treat or an admonishment. The reinforcement learning agent continually performs actions, evaluates if the reward/punishment received is satisfactory, and then acts again. This type of learning works especially well in learning optimised sequences of decisions, such as how a robot should move an assembly line, or how to announce a strategy during a game of chess. The system keeps trying out different strategies to see what actions would produce the best rewards over the sequence of steps.

Adaptability in AI

Adaptivity of AI is the capacity of an artificial system to adapt its behaviour to new inputs or changing environments. Such a capacity is essential for applications that are subject to unforeseeable changes in conditions, as is the case for autonomous vehicles navigating through traffic.

Machine Learning Models

At its centre, adaptability is based on the fact that the machine learning models that are at the core of all AI systems are gradually adaptive. That is, feedback from the environment modifies the parameter settings of these models to make internal representations better match what is happening 'out there'. A popular kind of model, known as neural networks, which are used in various forms in deep learning, modifies the values of the weights linking their neurons to make their output better match what is happening. The ability to modify the inner structures of neural networks is what makes it possible for AI adapt to various circumstances without a human constantly fine-tuning the parameters.

Transfer Learning

The second is transfer learning, by which an AI can adapt to a new task by importing knowledge from a previous task. The most common application of transfer learning is where knowledge about a task with one kind of data, such as spotting cars in photographs, is applied to another related task such as spotting trucks. When applying this approach, the AI would need to learn far less from the original data to apply its tools to the new task than it would if it were starting from scratch.

Challenges in AI Learning and Adaptation

While AI's ability to learn and adapt is impressive, it also presents significant challenges:

Data Dependency

AI systems are data-hungry, but it's often difficult and costly to collect large, high-quality unbiased data sets. And when the data that's used to train the AI system is flawed or biased, the system will make decisions according to those flaws.

Generalization

Being a good generaliser means being able to perform well on new data you have not seen before. Nevertheless, in a phenomenon known as overfitting, an AI can be very good at performing on its training data (ie, the training data it has learnt from), but poor on new data. Overcoming this difficulty and learning how much to fit the training data and how much to overfit it (ie, to perform only on the training data and never generalise out to new data) is one of the greatest challenges in AI.

Ethical and Societal Impact

It means that learning and adaptation by AI systems must also be ethical and socially responsible, ie, without entrenching or increasing unfair biases or inequalities. The problem will need not only continual attention, but also governance.

Conclusion

Gaining a better understanding of how these AI systems learn and adapt is crucial to making effective use of their abilities and helping ensure they're used ethically. This will require continued iterations of training, adaptation and control as the systems are developed and we interact with them. An ongoing challenge for developers and users alike will be how to empower these new intelligent technologies in a manner that's guided by accountability such that we can be assured that, as they continue to get smarter and smarter, they retain alignment with human values and social norms.

CHAPTER FOUR:
From Vision to Reality: Building an AI

There are many factors involved in bringing an AI system into existence, from weeks and months of brainstorming to the implementation stages. This chapter discusses the practicalities of AI development. It will look at the processes and technologies involved in creating an AI system, from collecting and preparing data to choosing the algorithms and implementing the system. All steps required for AI system creation are demonstrated in this chapter.

Step 1: Defining the Problem

Tell me what problem you're trying to solve, and I'll create an AI for it.

The first step to building an AI system is to clarify the problem it's trying to solve. What are your users trying to achieve? What are the relevant state variables, and what are the constraints under which the system will operate? A thoughtfully chosen problem statement informs a range of crucial design decisions, providing guidance on data, algorithms, and evaluation metrics. It also helps to ensure you build an AI that achieves any goals that matter. Do you want to make manufacturing more efficient? Enhance interactions with customers through chatbots? Diagnose disease through medical imaging?

Step 2: Data Collection and Preparation

Because AI systems 'learn' from data, this is perhaps the most important stage of the process – not to mention the most time-consuming. This is where data are sourced from practical, simulated and synthetic environments and prepared for 'training' an AI model. In this step, the data must be drawn from real-world contexts in an appropriate fashion and subsequently cleaned up and synthesised so that it is convenient to work with. In particular, there must be enough data for an AI model to make meaningful associations between inputs and outputs. Furthermore, this data must be unbiased and accurate so as not to affect the model's training.

For supervised learning models, this step also entails labelling the data at scale and that can require intensive human oversight and the expertise of domain experts. Data-augmentation tricks can make data sets artificially larger, say by modifying datasets to produce variants with a certain degree of randomness that improves models.

Step 3: Choosing the Right Algorithms

Getting the right algorithm will make the difference between a useful system and a clunker An AI system is certainly based on algorithms, but the software developer must choose the best algorithms for the job. That depends on the type of data available, and what exactly the problem is. How can one construct a system to respond to a question about existence? Common algorithmic options include decision trees, neural networks, support vector machines – and balancing a different set of trade-off issues for each. There will always be unavoidable mistakes built into the program, the choice depends on whether they are unclear or tedious to interpret (accuracy), whether they are easy to understand or explain (interpretability), or whether they can be quickly applied now of decision (computational efficiency).

However, developers are sometimes allowed to pool these algorithms in an ensemble method, which can improve performance: many weak models can thereby be combined into one (potentially) stronger, more robust, and more accurate predictive model.

Step 4: Training the Model

Armed with the data and the choice of algorithm, it's time to train the AI model. Here the data is 'fed' through the algorithm, and the model is allowed to learn the material over many successive iterations. The training process tunes the parameters in the model (e.g. the weights in a neural network) to minimise error and thus maximise accuracy.

Training could be computationally expensive and time-consuming for big datasets and a complex model, such as a deep learning network. However, one might leverage the potential of special hardware, such as graphics processing units (GPUs) and tensor processing units (TPUs), to speed up the process.

Step 5: Testing and Evaluation

Once a model is trained, a logical next step is to test it: check if it does what it's supposed to do. Often this is done on a set of data that was not among the sample used for training (hence the labels of test data and test set to denote this use). To measure how well the model performed, we look at its test accuracy, precision, recall, F1 score and so forth. During the testing phase, it might become apparent that the model is not working as intended, perhaps by overfitting: it solves the label prediction problem on the data used to train the model perfectly but performs badly on entirely new and unseen data.

Step 6: Integration and Deployment

The final component comprises bringing the AI system into the world where it will need to function – i.e., deploying the

AI model and integrating it across existing systems and workflows. Issues here could encompass how the AI interacts with other software, managing resources to run the system or secure the infrastructure required to do so.

There are also ongoing monitoring and hygiene measures required to account for shifts in the environment or data, as well as intermittent re-training to ensure the system remains accurate and relevant.

Conclusion

But it's structured; an AI system needs to be defined clearly, carefully prepared, managed strategically, tested relentlessly. And it needs to work, not just at the level of the component technology but also at the level of the larger system in which it is embedded. As AI continues to grow and mature, the techniques and technologies on which these stages rely are also growing and maturing.

CHAPTER FIVE:
AI in Action: Case Studies of Current Implementations

Because of sophisticated artificial intelligence (AI) technology, a plethora of applications can now be applied to a wide range of businesses and traditional ways of doing things. Problems that have existed throughout human history are being solving for the first was previously not possible. This chapter looks at how various businesses are now applying this technology in specific case studies. We are now faced with a real, tangible picture of modern-day AI thinking machines and how they are working today and transforming industries.

Healthcare: Diagnosing Diseases

Perhaps the most important medical application today is how it's being used to deliver diagnoses of disease with more accuracy than human experts. We have AI systems that can detect skin cancer, after being taught to identify the invisible patterns within an image of a skin lesion, perhaps indicating a malignant tumour – things that an expert's eye might miss. An oft-cited example is one published in 2016 in the journal Nature: an AI system's skill at spotting skin cancers matched that of specialist dermatologists, helping to detect disease earlier and therefore save lives.

Finance: Fraud Detection

The adoption of AI in the finance sector has been particularly pronounced. AI systems are trained to detect fraudulent behaviour by monitoring transactions of users and flagging behaviour that diverges from an established norm. For instance, financial institutions are using AI to analyse customer spending habits and scan for anomalies in spending patterns in real time. This alignment allows for fraudulent transactions to be discovered almost simultaneously when a cardholder transacts, and the fraudulent activity is midnight on the other end of the network. It not only helps the bank safeguard its assets, but also the customers by securing their financial safety and shield the customers from any harm.

Automotive: Autonomous Vehicles

Autonomous vehicles are the latest generation in a suite of AI application to emerge in the automotive industry. Companies such as Tesla, Waymo and Uber among others have been developing self-driving cars that leverage AI to build environmental precepts and make driving decisions. Many sensors (e.g., laser, optical, thermal, ultrasonic) and cameras are employed to pick up, detect and transmit data into AI systems that could potentially represent the environment, analyse, and predict the behaviour of other road users and guide the steering mechanism for autonomous driving. Besides reducing accidents, such systems are expected to improve traffic flow and dramatically transform transportation systems soon.

Retail: Personalized Recommendations

The retail industry has today been completely changed by AI because it can allow people to shop for the products they really want through some personalization. For instance, Amazon, a giant of E-commerce websites, have used AI to analyse what each individual customer needs. Amazon will continually feed various data of individual customers into AI algorithms, so that one day when one user sign in the website their AI algorithm will "create" a set of products that they may be interested in according to what they bought before, what they searched for, and items seen in the past, etc. Not only does this create a better experience for customers shopping online, making it easier and faster, but also the ability to advertise according to individuals' needs can bring more cash.

Agriculture: Precision Farming

On the farm, AI is used in what we call precision farming, where farmers use artificial intelligence to analyse data collected from multiple sources, such as satellite imagery, weather pattern predictions, or sensors planted in the field that sample soil conditions. These vast amounts of data are fed into an AI algorithm that informs the farmer on, for instance, optimal planting times and irrigation conditions, soil management and crop rotation, and pest and disease control. With the help of AI, farmers are able to make better decisions to increase yields, minimise waste and reduce the ecological footprint of farming.

Entertainment: Content Creation

For example, the entertainment industry uses AI to produce and personalise content. Movie studios use algorithms to analyse screenplays to pinpoint when and how scripts can be rewritten for greater box office success. Music streaming services such as Spotify use AI to analyse listening habits for better playlist curation and greater user engagement and satisfaction.

Conclusion

But they highlight just a handful of the thousands of ways AI is being implemented today in industries across the globe.

Each case reveals how AI technology could drastically transform current industries by enhancing their efficiency, precision, and personalisation, ultimately reshaping the nature of industry work. As AI continues to advance, it will likely deliver more applications and spur new innovations for global industries of the future. Surveying the examples of AI implementation not only demonstrates what AI thinking machines can do for us now, but also sets the stage for discussing what those machines mean for the rest of us.

CHAPTER SIX:
The Capabilities of AI: What AI Can and Cannot Do

Over recent decades, AI has gained many new abilities that hint at a world of even more spectacular, immersive, and useful tech. By now, we're all accustomed to AI's absurd infestations in many areas of work and life. This explosion of AI technologies has heralded the dawn of a new chapter in our history. But there are limits to what AI can do. Understanding those limits is key to unlocking AI's transformative power, while at the same time reminding us where it's out of its depth. This chapter is an exploration of what AI can, and cannot, possibly do.

Strengths of AI:

Speed and Efficiency

Some of AI's greatest strengths are that (i) it can make reliable decisions, and (ii) it can process and analyse much larger volumes of data than humans can.

It will be valuable where time is critical and sound short-term planning and rapid responses are necessary. Examples include high-speed financial trading, website search functions, drone piloting for complex tasks, and black-box AI systems that manage emergency response procedures. We have trained AI systems to do more data mining, pattern recognition and similar computational tasks, and now we can take advantage of their high-speed, large-data processing and analysis abilities.

Scalability

As they work at a faster rate, the error rate for ai systems remains steady or even drops – something that wouldn't be possible for human workers who get tired or less precise over time. This scaling up is a noteworthy advantage of ai over humans in many contexts, whether it's digital marketing or the analysis of consumer data, where enormous streams of information are generated daily.

Consistency and Reproducibility

Such systems are designed to follow algorithms. A simple way to define an algorithm is that it's any process that ensures consistency: if you do this the same way two times, it doesn't matter when you do it, the result will be the same. In humans, there are huge differences from each moment to each moment, while the algorithm itself doesn't change; it's designed to do something that doesn't depend on our subjectivity, our moods or other variations caused by different physical states. Humans are notoriously inconsistent actors; even award-winning chefs can cook substandard food on bad days. From a certain perspective, the essence of an algorithm is its reliability. It can be executed ad infinitum until the process becomes overturned by new, more precise algorithms – and even then, only slowly. This qualitative aspect of consistency is particularly important across a wide range of tasks and jobs, in sectors where error is not an option. Consistency is important in the manufacturing world, for instance, in supporting quality control.

Weaknesses of AI:

Lack of Generalization

Though AI systems are fast learning in narrow domains, they tend to fail at generalising, especially when faced with actions or narratives that deviate from their training data. It's a common problem to see how an AI can learn something in one context, but not another. For example, an AI trained to classify stop signs in broad daylight can become stumped by identically labelled images in fog. That's why AI learning fails to generalise across tasks, something humans typically do without much effort.

Absence of Emotional Intelligence

Emotional intelligence the ability to understand, interpret or respond to human emotion with the nuance that human beings bring to this process means that a computer lacks empathy and this in turn makes AI less effective than human beings at softer tasks that empathy plays a part in, such as nursing human beings back to mental health or helping to maintain a good relationship between a customer and the service they're using.

Ethical and Social Implications

As in, for example, using an artificial intelligence for hiring which is based on data that reflects historical ethnic biases in hiring, then the AI might show similar biases. These systems can incorporate biases reflected in its training data, and thus perpetuate discriminatory outcomes. This is a specific ethical concern for AI, and it requires continuous vigilance and incentives for checks and balances so that biases identifying one group over another are not built into an AI system.

Real-World Limitations:

Dependency on Data Quality

Performance depends to a large degree on how good the data is used to train them. But poor-quality data – incomplete datasets, wrong labels, or biased data – can seriously hamper an AI's performance, producing erroneous outputs and decisions.

Adaptability Challenges

Once deployed, AI systems generally lack the flexibility to adapt to new requirements or new environments without being extensively retrained or redesigned. Humans, by contrast, demonstrate flexibility and adaptability by learning to perform new tasks or changing strategies in response to new information in a far more fluid manner.

Conclusion

It's clear strengths and glaring weaknesses tell us what AI can and can't do, and whether it can and should replace or supplement other forms of intelligence. While AI bots are often marvels of technical accomplishment, they are only sometimes marvels of human accomplishment.

CHAPTER SEVEN:
Ethics and AI: Moral Considerations in AI Deployment

Given the increasing role that artificial intelligence (AI) technologies play in our institutions' daily operations, their ethical considerations have also increased in importance and weighing the moral implications of deploying AI systems can be pressing. Questions about fairness, privacy, accountability, and society's impact become central to AI evaluations. In this chapter, we'll explore some of the ethical quandaries that need to be navigated to ensure that AI technologies are beneficial for society and the people who use them and don't create or worsen existing issues.

Fairness and Bias

Another well-known ethical hazard linked to an AI scenario carries the promise of minimising certain kinds of human biases: inherent biases that could be programmed into AI systems by designing based on skewed data sets, flawed algorithms, or human interpretations. For example, racial bias in facial recognition technologies has caught public attention for higher error rates in detecting faces of certain racial backgrounds. Developers would have thought otherwise in designing the systems and data sets, but some still slip through. To mitigate the risk, developers carefully need to source diverse data sets for testing and validation by building some form of feedback mechanisms within the systems to catch biased outcomes over time. For artificial general intelligence to become truly general and useful, fairness must be specified from the beginning of the 'process stages' of the systems' design – and rigorously tested for, much like other risks – to ensure that algorithmic approximations of human performance don't lead to discrimination of various kinds.

Transparency and Explainability

Many of these AI systems, particularly those based on techniques like deep learning, are highly opaque, or 'black box'. It can be exceptionally difficult or impossible for a user or other person affected by the result to scrutinise why the AI reached its decision, and therefore to understand and overturn a decision that went astray or appears unfair. Scientists, researchers, and policymakers are exploring ways in which AI reasoning might be made fallible – or even more trustworthy and understandable to human observers. This could range from simplifying AI models for use in safety-critical applications or devising new standards of explainability.

Privacy Concerns

Many AI systems are driven by large amounts of data, some of which might also be very personal. Ethical deployment of AI would have to include some thinking about the collection, retention, and analysis of this data in relation to wider issues of privacy. Privacy-preserving techniques, such as anonymising, encrypting, or sanitising data, or forms of 'differential privacy' derived from information-theoretic and statistical experiments, fulfil an instrumental role when it comes to ensuring AI respects users' privacy and so upholds protections such as the GDPR in Europe.

Accountability

Unlike other technologies where accountability can be straightforward, for autonomous or semi-autonomous AI systems, it is much more difficult. It is imperative that accountability can be determined if an AI system decides to make a harm. Who is to blame? The developer? The user? The manufacturer? The AI itself? Strong legal and regulatory frameworks can help address problems of accountability, ensuring that victims can seek redress, and that there are incentives for actors bringing AI to market to ensure safety and ethical design.

Impact on Employment

When AI is used to automate tasks better than humans can do them – like on telecoms hotlines, or in manufacturing, or even when journalism is machine-generated — jobs will be destroyed. AI-enabled systems will replace humans in many jobs in manufacturing, transport, and administration. Those workers will need updating either skills-wise or position-wise. An ethically involved deployment will have to mitigate these impacts in foresighted ways (eg, retraining programmes, AI literacy education, or policies that create new jobs fit for human/AI 'symbiosis').

Societal and Cultural Impact

Besides its immediate applications, AI shapes the way society is organised, and cultural norms entrenched — for instance, recommendation systems tailoring feeds on social media can affect public opinion, political polarisation, and echo chambers. This means that ethical questions in AI must take a wider societal view — looking at the cultural dimensions in society and of technologies and aiming to shape positive outcomes.

Conclusion

These ethical questions related to the deployment of AI are not an afterthought – they are essential to the advance of AI into society, and the maturation of AI technologies will bring new ethical questions. Because it is so important that AI is not abused but is suspended in a web of moral guidelines for how it can be used, all of us – not just ethicists, not just technologists or policymakers, but also the public – must vigorously contribute to the effort to develop and integrate best practices for the ethical use of AI. Meeting these challenges responsibly will help ensure that we maintain our humanity even as the nature of work changes dramatically in the year ahead.

CHAPTER EIGHT:
Safeguarding Humanity: Controls and Safety in AI Design

The quick pace of innovation in artificial intelligence (AI) and the consequent integration of machine learning into more and more parts of society require us to develop a strong framework for assuring that such systems or their agents are safe, trustworthy and in control. In this chapter, we discuss the key controls and safety requirements that need to be developed and included in the design and development of AI systems to protect against the misuse of these systems and ensure that society benefits from the use of AI.

Understanding AI Safety

The field of AI safety includes a variety of technical approaches to address risks of unintended bad behaviour, both technical (i.e., bugs in software and security risks) and ethical (i.e., bad decisions that lead to bad outcomes).

Key Areas of Focus in AI Safety:

Robustness and Reliability

AI systems need to be resilient in the face of a wide range of inputs and conditions: that is, they should not, say, return a wrong decision in the face of unexpected inputs or data that are radically different from those in their training set. Stress testing, which involves applying extremes of conditions or data to systems, enables the identification of failure potentially in advance, as does the testing of reliability, which is a test that systems operate over an extended period under different conditions.

Security Measures

Just as with the rise of other powerful technologies, as we increase the use of AI systems, we will also increase the risk of malicious attackers who would try to leverage these systems for their own gain and nefarious purposes. Banks will have to be more vigilant in protecting their AI systems from attacks like data poisoning (for e.g., by feeding a trained AI bad data to misguide it) and adversarial attacks that design inputs to trick the AI into making decisional errors. Robust cryptography, secure authentication protocols, and intrusion detection systems are some of the first steps that can protect AI systems.

Fail-Safe Mechanisms

Fail-safe mechanisms allow an AI system to be offloaded quickly or shut down entirely if it begins to run amok or 'leak' into parts of the world where it's not allowed to go. Examples include manual overrides, automatic shut-off mechanisms, redundancy functions that maintain certain key functions even when a part of the system fails, etc.

Transparency and Traceability

This requires the fact that AI systems can give an account of what led to a particular decision and to be able to trace back through the logic chain all the way to the inputs if something goes wrong. Without this sort of traceability, the opportunities for debugging and improving the system – or for rebuilding trust among users and regulators should things go awry – are lost.

Ethical Design

We should responsibly bring ethical concerns in the design of AI systems, for instance by designing AI to be principled. Principled design means feeding ethical principles (such as fairness, accountability, or respect for user privacy) in the design and development of AI systems. Principled design also means engaging stakeholders in the development of an AI system, and trying to understand how diverse humans and their values can contribute to more comprehensive safety and control issues.

Regulatory Compliance

Lakkaraj also emphasises the importance of following both local and international regulations, which include staying abreast of new rules on AI as they develop, and making sure any systems adhere to all laws and standards that apply. Standards could include privacy rules for data protection and consumer protection, or AI-specific standards for certain applications such as healthcare or transportation.

Scenario Planning and Risk Assessment

We need to think what we can do now to mitigate those failures or misuses before they occur. An obvious approach is scenario planning: drawing up lists of future scenarios, including the worst-case scenarios, and defining what we can do now that might reduce the chances of those scenarios coming about. Existing risk assessment frameworks can be checked against the likelihood and impact of such risks, to ensure that our assessment of safety steps is well-founded and in proportion.

Conclusion

Protecting humanity from AI risks is not just a 'do it once and be done' task; it's a complex, evolving, and iterative process that has to change and adapt with AI itself. This is a task for AI developers, policymakers, ethicists, as well as AI deployers, end-users, and others involved in advancing AI's growth. Through stringent, adaptable control and safety mechanisms in design, as well as ethically sound and responsibly designed AI systems of regulatory compliance, we can gain access to the benefits of AI while successfully mitigating the risks. Dedication to safety and ethical design in AI will be crucial for creating technologies that are beneficial to society and that receive the trust of the public and other AI stakeholders.

CHAPTER NINE:
Regulation and Policy: Governing the Power of AI

Since AI technology is expected to become more ubiquitous and influential in every sphere of life, it demands the same form of regulation and policy-making that regulates everything else. This chapter studies the way regulatory regimes are first built and subsequently enforced as the deployment of AI systems assumes significant influence over the functioning of our society and technology. The aim is to safeguard the public interest simultaneously with encouraging innovation and growth in the field of AI.

The Need for AI Regulation

AI systems and the technologies driving them will likely improve our lives in many ways, from greater efficiency to better decision-making to new inventions of all kinds. But AI will also introduce novel and compelling considerations related to privacy, security, fairness, and accountability. The public needs effective regulation of these systems for the benefits to outweigh the risks of potential harms from AI.

Key Areas of Focus in AI Regulation:

Privacy and Data Protection

The treatment of privacy has special significance in the context of AI, given that these systems often draw on big datasets of personal information. Here, frameworks of data protection – such as the regulations introduced in the European Union through the General Data Protection Regulation – play an important role. The GDPR sets out rights linked to the processing of personal data, including the rights to consent, to be erased, and to be informed, all of which are important here, in the context of AI systems. In this way, the regulation of AI can ensure that relevant privacy norms are respected and that data-related practices are 'secure and transparent', as the Word Excel lawyer requested.

Fairness and Non-discrimination

If AI systems are trained on tainted data sets, they will perpetuate, if not exponentially aggravate, biases; regulations must demand that AI systems work in a fair, non-discriminatory manner, and there must be standards to monitor and eliminate bias. This includes standards for how AI is developed, trained, and deployed.

Accountability and Transparency

Standards must, more specifically, establish boundaries for accountability and transparency in AI operations, ensuring that, at all times, there is a clear line of accountability, wherever and whenever a given AI system fails or hurts anyone. Further, requirements for explainability – that is, making it possible for an AI to make its decision intelligible to humans – should also be required. These would go hand-in-hand with the first point, insofar as they could foster public trust and enable the proliferation of a more ethically exploitable AI technology.

Safety and Security

Physical and cybersecurity is another category of risk for AI regulations. This covers problems such as standards for the robustness and reliability of AI systems, and protections to prevent cyber-attacks that could require control systems to take actions that they should not.

Developing AI Regulations

However, comprehensive AI regulation is difficult to achieve, for technological development often moves faster than policies are made. It requires a synergistic engagement of various stakeholders, including AI developers, users, ethicists, and the general public.

Multi-stakeholder Involvement

Good regulation involves hearing from a wide array of stakeholders, including technologists who know what can and cannot be done with AI, business leaders who understand the economic incentives, legal scholars who know the regulatory implications, and citizens impacted by the technologies.

Flexible and Adaptive Frameworks

Since AI technology is constantly changing, regulations must be responsive and agile to adjust as, and when, subsequent generations of the technology are introduced and affect the world in different ways. Sandboxing – testing AI systems in real-world environments under controlled scenarios – and iterative regulations that incorporate revisions and adjustments over stages of implementation are two examples of how agility can be introduced into regulatory processes.

International Collaboration

Because AI technology operates across borders, in order to regulate it properly, we need to engage in international cooperation. We need to co-ordinate regulation across multiple jurisdictions so that we do not end up with a regulatory patchwork incompatible with international cooperation and trade.

Conclusion

That's where policy comes into play. By setting AI systems to operate in ways that are reliable, fair and trustworthy, regulation allows AI technology to reach its fullest potential. As we increase the number and sophistication of ways in which we embed AI into the social and economic fabric, the development of nuanced, inclusive, agile regulatory systems will be critical to the success and societal acceptance of the technology. Striking the right balance between invention and vigilance will enable AI to be the greatest boon possible for humanity, promoting the public good rather than undermining it.

CHAPTER TEN:
Preventing AI Autonomy: Techniques to Maintain Control

As artificial intelligence (AI) systems grow more powerful and autonomous, safeguarding our ability to keep these technologies under human control – to ensure that AI systems continue to serve our legitimate interests and respect our fundamental values – takes on growing importance. This chapter discusses several techniques and approaches that people are developing to avoid the risk of unintended (and undesired) AI autonomy, so that AI systems do not escape the bounds of their beneficial design.

Understanding AI Autonomy

'AI autonomy' describes AI systems with the capacity to accomplish tasks or make decisions without human intervention. Greater autonomy for an AI system could indeed improve its functionality and effectiveness, but it also brings up serious questions about who and what stays in control, and in what way. The challenge is to create AI systems that can be as highly functional as possible without becoming dangerously out of control.

Techniques to Maintain Control Over AI:

Hierarchical Control Systems

One way to maintain more control is simply to structure the system as a hierarchy of control, whereby things that could be done with no human input would first be decided by humans. For example, lower-level decisions, like what to do after a low-level alarm, can be fully automated so that they are handled only by the AI system. High-impact decisions, like re-routing important vehicles, travel, or onsite personnel, would be escalated back to the human operators. That way, AI would not be allowed to decide without direct human input things that have the potential to have a large impact.

Designing for Auditability

You need auditable AI systems that are designed from the ground up to be monitored and reviewed, so that decisions are transparent. When you understand how decisions are made, you're in a much better position to oversee them. This is where audit trails can help a great deal: records are kept of every step that an AI system has made and the rationale behind its decisions. Of course, it's always preferable to monitor the activity of an AI system as it goes along. But if something goes wrong, such as a chatbot going rogue or an autonomous weapons system targeting civilians, the audit trails will be invaluable for a retrospective analysis.

Safe Exploration

Through reinforcement learning, AI systems learn from their interactions with the world. The corollary of not having direct experience with the world oneself, however, is that strange and dangerous behaviours can emerge from learning – the primary consideration in Safe-AI's research. To avoid these issues, safe exploration techniques are necessary to encourage effective learning by ensuring that AI systems explore their environments, and learn new tasks properly, without hitting any safety boundaries or resulting in harm. Achieving this might involve teaching AI systems using virtual training environments, learning in simulation, and building safety constraints into the learning process.

Use of Ethical and Normative Frameworks

Embedding ethical and normative frames into AI design can guide AI decision-making by imbuing it with the values and norms that ground decisions in human standards of rightness and value. Developers can program AI with explicit rules or value systems or can code 'learning algorithms' that observe human conduct, or that learn via feedback from human input.

Redundancy and Fail-Safes

The principle of redundancy can be applied in cases where multiple levels or copies of AI systems are created, in order to compensate for any system failures and prevent unintended autonomous action if one level fails. Such systems should be designed to stop (fail-safe) as soon as they go outside of their intended domain. Examples include the automatic stopping or deactivation of such a system when it reaches certain parameters, or through a manual stop of a rogue system, using the appropriate human operator interface.

Challenges in Preventing AI Autonomy:

Balancing Autonomy and Control

Getting this balance right – making optimal use of AI autonomy without unwarrantedly sacrificing sufficient human control – is difficult. On the one hand, delegating executive control to AI could raise the risks of genuine harms or malicious uses, but, on the other hand, unwarrantedly resisting AI control to preserve human control could substantially diminish the productivity and efficiency of AI systems.

Technological and Ethical Complexity

The technologies in play are often fraught: they are likely to be (and will need to be) complicated, and highly differentiated in ways that don't exist currently, thereby making the application of control mechanisms technically complex. They raise ethical challenges in the form of disagreement about what counts as adequate control, and so face a consent-building challenge in their application.

Conclusion

We, as humans, have the power to enshrine hierarchical control systems, ensure that AI systems are equally designed for auditability, build in safe methods of exploration, and develop techniques of AI that accurately represent the ethical frameworks we find important. As the technology evolves, and as new concerns present themselves, we must be willing to continually recalibrate the techniques that enable us to exert appropriate levels of control. The ethical future we seek – in which humans wield the power to guide AI towards aligning with our expectations.

CHAPTER ELEVEN:
AI and Employment: Navigating Job Disruption

With the integration of artificial intelligence (AI) into all sectors of industry, it is not only transforming the way that the business landscape works, but also the way that its workforce does as well. In this chapter, we analyse the dual role of AI in work: as both a creator and destroyer. This is fundamental to develop policies to reduce its damaging effects or use it to its fullest potential, improving the workforce.

The Impact of AI on Jobs

We can see AI's influence over employment in two ways that are very different from but also dependent on one another: job creation and job destruction.

Job Displacement

AI and automation technologies could then do many of the things that humans are good at, just more efficiently: in manufacturing, robots can replace human workers in assembly line roles. It doesn't get the breaks or the repetitive strain injuries that humans do. In services, software that learns how to book appointments, process transactions, or read and mark data entry, could replace what were previously clerical roles.

The greatest risk of displacement is in sectors that involve heavy concentrations of routine manual and cognitive work. McKinsey Company research has found that the most vulnerable occupations are those associated with routine physical activities in highly predictable and structured environments, such as driving a truck or picking fruit, along with data collection and processing work.

Job Creation

Meanwhile, AI also creates jobs, both directly and indirectly. Direct jobs entail the development, maintenance, and evaluation of AI systems, which creates new, ongoing positions for AI specialists, data scientists, ethicists, user experience designers and other new roles. Indirect jobs that AI creates include new business services and industries stemming from entirely new technological products. For instance, autonomous driving technology not only creates demand for AI and robotics experts, but also for new services, such as remote vehicle operation and advanced vehicle maintenance.

Navigating the Transition

The challenge for society is not just to react to dislocations but to anticipate the transition in the labour market that AI is turbocharging.

Skills Development

In this process, there emerges a need for abilities that are harder to replicate using AI, such as emotional intelligence, creative problem-solving and strategic thinking. These are skills that the existing workforce and the workforce of the future could acquire through education and training. This could be through formal education systems, but also through on-the-job training and continuous professional development, to adapt to ever-changing job markets.

Policy Interventions

Governments have a role to play in helping to smooth the transition away from many current jobs. Possibilities include:

- **Safety Nets:** By introducing, or expanding, safety nets for AI-displaced workers like unemployment insurance and on-the-job training programmes.

- **Incentivise reskilling:** Tax incentives or subsidies for firms that invest in retraining employees for new roles.

– **Regulation:** Putting rules in place to govern just how and where AI is deployed, including ensuring that its use is handled ethically, and that it does not replace jobs in a mass way.

Promoting Entrepreneurship

This includes not just more jobs and new kinds of opportunities for entrepreneurs to start-up businesses, but it makes a lot of entirely new jobs possible as well. Lowering the barriers to entry in all of these fields make it possible for entrepreneurs to provide new services and products that up to now have not been possible, and incubators, grants and mentor programmes to nurture that innovation could create many new jobs and help to diversify our economy.

Conclusion

We must embrace that duality because the effects of AI on the future of work are substantial and multi-layered. As a force of automation, AI could and likely will displace many jobs. Therefore, the second approach needs to be on how to deal with job displacements, both physical and social. But AI can also be a force of creation and enhancement. With the right skills, policy interventions and culture of experimentation and creative destruction conducive to innovation and entrepreneurship, the arts of the machine age can help societies prepare in a systemic manner how to fend off the worst effects of automation and maximise the best. This is how we will construct a workforce that can operate in the age of intelligent machines.

CHAPTER TWELVE:
Balancing Power: AI in National Security

Artificial intelligence (AI) is recognised as having considerable potential to transform national security practices around the world. As states begin to integrate AI technologies into their security practices as part of the security-by-algorithm paradigm, there will be consequences for protection, as well as a great deal of complexity arising from issues around control, ethics and global stability. The purpose of this chapter is to explore the power politics of AI in national security. Every new technology brings new possibilities and new challenges for the power politics of international relations. AI, however, may present even greater transformative effects. While the current emphasis is on military use, defined broadly to include law enforcement, the question for this chapter is how AI will reshape the 'matrix of power' between states and, therefore, the zone of interaction between them. Importantly, what will be needed to maintain that balance and avoid creating a new site for instability in the international order?

The Role of AI in National Security

AI technologies are being employed throughout the realm of national security, from intelligence collection and analysis to fully autonomous systems to cybersecurity defences.

Intelligence and Surveillance

AI dramatically boosts the capabilities of intelligence operations. Flowing through sophisticated all-source search engines rapidly, data is turned into actionable intelligence that syncs well with strategic planning. AI algorithms can trawl reams of satellite imagery to track military movements or construction of facilities, often in real time.

Autonomous Weapons

Possibly the most controversial AI application in national security is in the field of autonomous weapon systems, which can strike targets without a human pulling the trigger. While supporters believe that autonomous weapons can lower the overall number of casualties among combatants by reducing collateral damage and unnecessary human error, critics fear that they could lower the barrier to routine armed conflict, as well as lead to unintended escalations of violence.

Cybersecurity

AI is both a dual-use and a boost for cyber defences as well as for cyber offence, for example, AI systems can help defenders detect and neutralise attacks more quickly than human controllers can. But the same computing power can be leveraged for more complex and cunning cyber-attacks, setting off a cycle, an arms race between cyber defences and offences.

Challenges and Risks

Integrating AI into national security strategies are destabilising implications that must be managed to avoid further fueling geopolitical tensions.

Ethical Concerns

AI in national security comes with huge ethical issues, particularly the tension between who makes autonomous lethal decisions, and who gets to be shrivelled. Clear ethical frameworks and international treaties are necessary to genuinely legalise the use of AI for such issues. The use of AI must be ethically justifiable and abide by the rule of law.

Security Dilemmas

Security dilemmas would also be at play, as one state's advancement in AI-driven defence technologies catalyses other states either to acquire the same technological capabilities, or else suffer a loss of security relative to their strategic competitors. Arms races could ensue, destabilising international relations, and lowering the bar of escalation in general. Tensions could increase the temptation for a 'use it or lose it' mentality.

Control and Accountability

Racing down the road in a military engagement might be an inopportune time to find the AI system making its own decisions. Whatever the driving scenario we could imagine, it's vital to have testing and robust control. It's also vital to have accountability, so that we can recognise when the system does indeed go off road, when it stumbles into a tricky situation, or (the worst nightmare) when it causes a failure or an accident. And when we're not driving together, decisions are being made by or with the help of AI that might have far-reaching consequences. We need to be sure that those decisions are being made in the right way, with clear accountability.

Strategies for Balance and Stability

Ultimately, there are some steps that can be taken to address these challenges and ensure that national security AI is a net positive for international stability.

International Cooperation and Regulation

This would require setting up international norms and standards regarding the application of AI in national security, including treaties and agreements that set out permissible uses of AI technologies and international monitoring of compliance. It could also involve international cooperation that leads to the possibility of sharing best practices regarding how to manage AI's risks.

Transparency and Confidence-Building Measures

Enhancing the transparency of AI systems for national-security applications could build trust among countries – as could confidence-building measures such as shared standards and joint exercises. Suspicions could also be diminished and misperceptions that could lead to conflict could be prevented.

Continuous Oversight and Evaluation

AI programmes must be subject to continuing oversight to make sure they maintain ethical and strategic foundations, such as by regularly conducting risk assessments of AI systems to check their effects on stability and resilience and amending policies to account for any new risks.

Conclusion

The growing integration of AI is changing the goals and means of national security and creating new opportunities and dangers. Is there a way to balance optimising the benefits of AI's ability to accomplish important security objectives with the need to do so in a way that promotes ethics, good governance, and international stability? The answers to these questions will determine how nations prepare for the future of conflict and peace.

CHAPTER THIRTEEN:
Public Perception and Media: Shaping the AI Narrative

Public perception of AI has a direct bearing on whether and how this technology is accepted and regulated. Media plays an important role in shaping public perception of AI. How people come to understand, feel about, and expect the future of AI will be shaped by how news and entertainment media construct stories about AI. This chapter will examine the resonance between public perception, media narratives and AI technology, to explore how the three elements mutually shape each other and ultimately influence the acceptance and regulation of AI.

The Influence of Media on AI Perceptions

When it comes to the media, coverage can feature stories of utopian futures where AI is a boon to humanity, or futures of great terror where it's taken over and humans are no longer in charge. Often, the characterisation of AI in the news, on film, in books and stories, and other media can go a long way to shaping public understanding and sentiment about the technology.

Highlighting Benefits and Innovations

These stories, always positive, stress the expediency, pliability and life-enriching prospects of AI. Success stories come from areas such medicinal health, in which AI can be used for diagnosing with a greater level of accuracy; or environmental science, in which AI supports in monitoring and countering climate change.

Addressing Risks and Challenges

At the same time, news coverage can illuminate real threats and ethical quandaries in the world of AI. Some anxiety can be fomented when stories highlight future job losses because of automation, or the ways that AI systems can incorporate bias, or invasion of privacy due to surveillance technologies, and so on. This type of coverage is important, too, because it lends a more balanced perspective on AI and promotes public discussion about necessary limitations on its deployment.

Public Engagement and Education

Public education is key to make AI less mysterious, and hopefully fostering a richer public debate, such that it can better adapt to a new era that everyday people might not have fully digested, yet. In other words, education and outreach is imperative to help reduce the epistemic distance between the complex aforementioned AI technologies and our everyday-full knowledge architecture, so that it can render us opinion-maker about the role that AI plays in our society.

Educational Programs

AI could be included in educational curricula up to and including tertiary education, as well as STEM (science, technology, engineering and mathematics) education for younger people. As far as possible, this should aim to foster the intellectual development of future generations wishing to engage with AI critically. Thirdly, establishing public seminars, workshops and open courses on AI that are made available to the public would go some way towards demystifying the technology and debunking myths propagated through the sensationalist media.

Public Dialogues and Consultations

Such engagement via dialogues and consultations can help build public trust and gather mentality from the bottom up, allowing citizens to raise their concerns and ask questions – and assuring that AI policies are shaped by the people whose lives are affected by these policies.

Media Responsibility and Ethical Reporting

As a gateway of knowledge and the most prevalent source of information in modern society, it is essential that media entities maintain the highest standards of journalistic and creative integrity to ensure that AI is reported upon responsibly.

Balanced Reporting

A sensible reporting approach should focus on balanced coverage that gives a sense of what is working well with AI, where it's having impacts, and what these might be; but it should also examine critically where things are going wrong and who stands to be most threatened. This would contribute to a lay understanding of the AI phenomenon.

Avoiding Sensationalism

Sensationalism is a problem with the complexity of AI, because there is an incentive to exaggerate either capabilities or threat for ratings or subscriptions as a sensationalist story. Media needs to avoid sensationalism and provide careful, information to prevent misinformation and hysteria.

Conclusion

The ongoing public discourse about the interface between AI and humans, the media spotlight, and the decisions taken by the regulators and policy-makers all combine in the continual shaping of our thoughts and understanding about AI. These enable or impede widespread and effective adoption of AI in our daily lives and work. Good public communication about AI, responsible media reportage and amplification, and public engagement that encourage a well-informed public to participate meaningfully in public debates and decision-making will all be important in the widespread adoption of AI in society. As AI becomes more established and embedded in various aspects of our daily life, ensuring that the public is informed, engaged and positive will be important for us to reap benefit from AI and overcome genuine concerns and challenges.

CHAPTER FOURTEEN:
Future Predictions: Where AI is Heading

As we consider the potential pathways for artificial intelligence (AI) in the future, it would be useful to anticipate what might be the developments in AI technology. This chapter provides an overview for potential future developments in the AI area; firstly, with the view of new trends of technologies, then the future projections followed by the broad perspective of human society can be envisioned. Understanding such pathways could provide some insights for those stakeholders preparing for the impacts from AI and ensuring that these technologies could conform to human societal inclination.

Technological Advancements

In tandem with explosive progress in AI algorithms, computing power, and data availability, the trajectory of AI development is fast-tracking there will be no stopping future progress. The implications are profound, for the world of work and beyond.

General AI

Even in the most complex AI systems of today, we can still consider them narrow-AI systems, meaning they are good at one task, but are unable to generalise their learning to new domains in the way that a human would. The driving motivation for AI research is actually to one day achieve Artificial General Intelligence, or AGI – an AI system that is able to play the role of general intelligence and learn and apply it to many domains independently. Such an AI could finally revolutionise our applications by building systems that could solve all manner of complex tasks on their own.

Quantum Computing and AI

Through this amazing speed in calculation steps, we are hoping that quantum computing will have a transformative effect on the way in which we process information. For AI, quantum computing could help machine learning algorithms with better optimisation and pattern-recognition capabilities, which might open the door to solving new types of problems that are currently out of reach for traditional computer architectures.

Economic and Social Shifts

AI will be rapidly integrated into economies and societies around the world, changing industries, workloads, and public lives.

Economic Transformation

Of course, AI is likely to widen economic divides, not only by eliminating jobs, but also by creating new markets and industries. For example, diagnostic services based on medical AI, individually tailored education or automated legal services are likely areas of growth, where improved services become more accessible and cheaper for a larger crowd.

Workforce Evolution

Rather, the combination of automation and the availability of large quantities of information means that the human workforce will need to shift to jobs that do not lend themselves as well to repetition. Those jobs – involving more creativity, strategy, and interpersonal interactions – will be more likely to leverage the capabilities of humans that are hardest to replicate through AI. In turn, education and training schemes will need to adapt to the new job 'forces', supporting different skill sets.

Ethical and Governance Challenges

But as it does so, and as AI advances and brings new opportunities for the betterment and harm of humankind, the associated ethical and governance issues will grow in complexity and immediacy.

Ensuring Ethical Alignment

Unless the emerging AI systems themselves become more advanced, their deployment will require new, more sophisticated safeguards not just to make them technically robust, but also to build in sufficient human-like ethical accountability, the driving force of which will need to originate from the regulatory framework itself. These safeguards would not only extend to technical systems but would call for engendering a more conscientious (and votes-inducing) dialogue between citizens and their governments on the ethics and public health benefits of algorithmic decision-making.

Global Governance

But because AI technology is both global and significant, we can't decide what to do alone. Instead, we'll need to set global standards and rules. We might also have to decide how we want to prioritise AI development, and therefore its uses. Because of the nature of capitalism and how it tends to concentrate resources — with the richest countries and individuals having the most money and seemingly the most power – it's likely that there will be large differences in AI development and access, both within and between rich and poor areas of the world. Even more reason, then, to aim for global governance of AI, so that any benefits can be widely shared, and AI doesn't widen the global inequality gap.

Speculative Futures

All the speculative ideas are just science fiction, even when they aren't – and even if they hold a kernel of truth within. Looking farther into the future, the imaginary scenarios involving artificial intelligence are just as mixed, with cautionary tales of AI becoming conscious alongside more comforting visions of AI as cooperative humans. Pervading these speculations is a mood of uncertainty, that we do not fully grasp what we are creating.

Conclusion

The long-term trajectories described in this paper have significant uncertainties and variations. They are not prophesies of the future, but rather a heuristic for charting a set of possible futures that would enable multi-stakeholder engagement on AI and the choices we need to make now to help shape the future. Stakeholders in technology firms, business, government, academia, and civil society have a critical role to play in this ongoing dialogue and collaboration. By identifying future changes and preparing responsibly, we can ensure that AI develops in ways that expand our capabilities, and improves daily life in the world, and help avoid the pitfalls where progress runs amok and amplifies new dangers. As we enter the co-evolution of human and AI futures, we must focus keenly on shaping how we can harness the power of AI to serve the public interest and address the challenges of our time.

CHAPTER FIFTEEN:
Conclusion: Controlling Our Creations

At the threshold of a new, artificial intelligence (AI) age, we might be justifiably thrilled at its awesome potential and afraid of where it might take us. The preceding chapters have examined the technological and social/ethical underpinnings of AI and assessed its potential benefits and drawbacks across a range of realms including ground-breaking national security applications, its likely effect on jobs, and the urgent questions of ethics we are currently grappling with. This final chapter synthesises these findings to yield significant conclusions about how to embrace AI in a manner that keeps humanity in the driver's seat of this inherently human technology.

Reaffirming Human Oversight

Indeed, the anxiety that runs through every layer of AI is the precariousness of retaining human control. The higher stakes that flow from making autonomous systems more deterministic and moving AI entities into higher- and-higher stakes decisions only intensify this anxiety and risk. As we have seen, the terms of hierarchical control systems, auditability, and ethics, which might otherwise seem like technical safeguards, are ultimate guarantees that AI does not stray from supporting and advancing human needs and values. It will remain an ongoing challenge to maintain such control. But no plan to develop AI can proceed in a meaningful way without embedding them into every stage of AI's development and operation.

Balancing Innovation with Caution

Pushing boundaries and innovating must be balanced with safeguards that reduce the chances of unintended consequences. The history of technological innovation is littered with examples where the pressures of advancement

– and perhaps competition – saw the adoption and use of specific technologies occur too quickly for questions of safety, or ethics, or consequences for society generally to be fully considered. This is particularly the case for AI because of its ever-expanding power and its ever-widening reach. A precautionary approach is rarely if ever an effective brake on innovation. Instead, it can help redirect us towards a responsible path that takes account of long-term consequences and harnesses a robust safety net.

Promoting Equity and Accessibility

AI might prove to be the bedrock of huge societal and economic changes – but also of dystopias if the risks of greater polarisation of wealth and work are left unchecked. Investing now in ways that justify people's trust in the potential of AI – from preventing polarisation of the job market with policy interventions, to international cooperation (to minimise geographical polarisation and create a fair playing field for adoption of technology across the globe) to training and education programmes to across-the-board revamp and retraining in work to ensure people are equipped for life in a new AI-augmented economy.

Strengthening Global Cooperation

The great challenges and opportunities presented by AI are not bound by national borders. From protecting data privacy, to cyber security, to controlling the use of autonomous weapons, there is a pressing need for coordination at an international level to prevent adverse outcomes and mitigate against them. International norms, treaties and regulatory frameworks will be key to ensuring that the development and use of AI are safe, secure, and equitable. Global cooperation will ensure that we can share the benefits and positive applications of AI, and that countries at different stages of taking up AI can learn from each other, preventing larger gaps in development across the globe.

The Role of Public Engagement

Ultimately, public perceptions matter, and they impact what actually happens. It's important for AI's potential to be realised – for the benefits of AI to be realised and limitations acknowledged. While computational power for machine learning is attracting significant investment, it's not everything. Addressing the public's concerns involves greater transparency about the capabilities (and limitations) of AI, and about how AI could influence and affect different people. This, in turn, depends on ensuring adequate opportunities for genuine public participation in AI's regulation and application. If we're going to democratise AI governance, we need to know what the people themselves think.

Envisioning the Future

AI is just starting to fundamentally change our world in ways that are difficult to imagine now. The hope is that AI will co-evolve with humanity in beneficial ways. To make this happen, we have a responsibility to choose our path, a path that considers that our creations may outlast and outperform us. We can do this by embedding human-centric values into its evolutionary path, by fostering an open and forward-looking culture, and by maintaining strong controls over AI systems. In this way, these systems can augment, not diminish, the human experience.

Final Thoughts

If the present generation of AI fails to live up to the ideals that we have for it, the story will be yet another truth: with great power comes great responsibility. Modern AI represents our intellectual hopes for the future. So, too, does it reflect our ethical and moral values. If we insist, and if we insist early enough, on guiding it along the right path, then our use of technology will continue to make the world less brutal, not more. By controlling our machines, we are controlling our future. We will make it one where we can continue to set the terms to make the technology serve humanity, not the reverse.

All Books Published By Author of This Book

These books can be viewed/ bought by following the link below to the Amazon site:

https://selvasmail.com/selvasbooks

Alternatively, should you wish to view the books on your phone or tablet, you could scan the barcode below, which will also take you direct to the Amazon site.

BOOKS ON WELLNESS & HEALTH (7 BOOKS)

BOOKS ON ALZHEIMER'S & DEMENTIA (5 BOOKS)

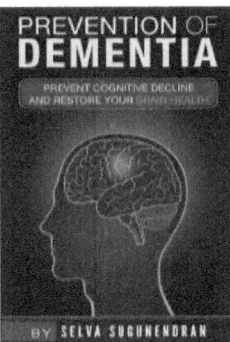
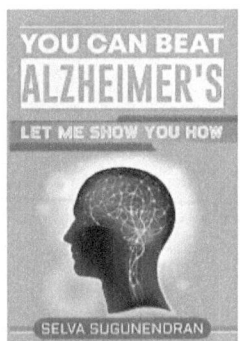

BOOKS ON SUCCESS (5 Books)

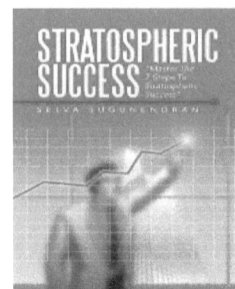

BOOKS ON AI (3 more to follow)

CHRISTIAN BOOKS (15 BOOKS)

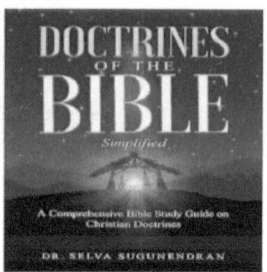

NEW ADDITIONS

APPENDICES

1. WEBSITE LINKS

http://MyChristianLifestyle.org

http://BlessMeLord.com

http://HealMeLord.today

http://CreationEvolutionAndScience.com

http://AIRoboticsForGood.com

http://DementiaAdvice.care

http://HowToLeadAVibrantLifeWithAlzheimers.com

http://PreventDelayReverseAlzheimers.com

2. CONTACT LINKS:

The Author: Selva@MyChristianLifestyle.org

All Books by Author Available on Amazon:
http://Books.Selvamedia.com

www.ingramcontent.com/pod-product-compliance
Lightning Source LLC
Chambersburg PA
CBHW031430210526
45464CB00005B/2129